My Five Super Senses
I FEEL IT!

Theresa Emminizer

PowerKiDS press

I use my skin
to touch and feel!

Some things I touch feel smooth.

Some things I touch feel bumpy.

I touch the grass.
It tickles!

The water feels wet
on my hands!

The sand feels dry on my feet.

I touch the snow.

It feels cold!

My mom's hand feels warm.

Some things I touch feel soft.

Some things I touch feel hard.

There are so
many things
to touch and feel!

Published in 2024 by The Rosen Publishing Group, Inc.
2544 Clinton Street, Buffalo, NY 14224

First Edition

Editor: Theresa Emminizer
Book Design: Rachel Rising

Photo Credits: Cover, p. 1 AnneMS/Shutterstock.com; p. 3 GOLFX/Shutterstock.com; pp. 5, 23 wavebreakmedia/Shutterstock.com; p. 7 Anna Kraynova/Shutterstock.com; p. 9 Tetiana Yablokova/Shutterstock.com; p. 11 Lia_Skyfox/Shutterstock.com; p.13 Valeriaya_Merzlikina/Shutterstock.com; p. 15 Mariia Andreeva/Shutterstock.com; p. 17 kiatipol2495/Shutterstock.com; p. 19 kdshutterman/Shutterstock.com; p. 21 Allgord/Shutterstock.com.

Library of Congress Cataloging-in-Publication Data

Names: Emminizer, Theresa, author.
Title: I feel it! / Theresa Emminizer.
Description: [Buffalo, New York] : PowerKids Press, [2023] | Series: My
    five super senses | Audience: Grades K-1
Identifiers: LCCN 2023033261 (print) | LCCN 2023033262 (ebook) | ISBN
    9781499443295 (library binding) | ISBN 9781499443288 (paperback) | ISBN
    9781499443301 (ebook)
Subjects: LCSH: Touch–Juvenile literature. | Senses and
    sensation–Juvenile literature.
Classification: LCC QP451 .E46 2023 (print) | LCC QP451 (ebook) | DDC
    612.8/8–dc23/eng/20230726
LC record available at https://lccn.loc.gov/2023033261
LC ebook record available at https://lccn.loc.gov/2023033262

Manufactured in the United States of America

Some of the images in this book illustrate individuals who are models. The depictions do not imply actual situations or events.

CPSIA Compliance Information: Batch #CWPK24 For further information contact Rosen Publishing at 1-800-237-9932.

Find us on

PK Beginners

Titles in This Series

I FEEL IT!

I HEAR IT!

I SEE IT!

I SMELL IT!

I TASTE IT!

PowerKiDS press™

ISBN: 9781499443288

9 781499 443288